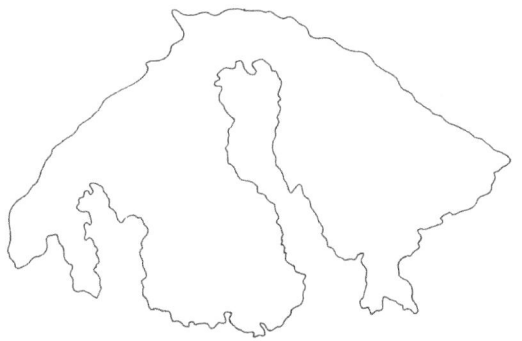

Text Copyright © 2022 Edee Kulper
Photography Copyright © 2022 Edee Kulper

This book's accompanying blog can be found at
www.lifeonorcasisland.com

Cover, layout, and interior design by Kayleigh Jankowski
Editing by Donna Lane and Molly Johnson

All rights reserved. No part of this book or its blog may be reproduced, transmitted, or stored in an information retrieval system in any form or by any means—graphic, electronic, or mechanical—without prior written permission from the author.

Use of Moran State Park images granted by Washington State Parks.

Use of preserve images (some whose locations are intentionally unspecified) granted by the San Juan County Land Bank.
The San Juan County Land Bank is a local land conservation program created by voters in 1990 and funded by a 1% real estate excise tax paid by purchasers of property in San Juan County. Through conservation easements or outright purchases, the Land Bank protects special places in the islands including coastlines, farmland, forests, and wetlands. For more information, contact the Land Bank at 360-378-4402 or visit www.sjclandbank.org.

The author made every effort to contact all people and places shown and/or mentioned in this book.

Front cover: The view from Eastsound on a spring day, with crystal clarity in both sky and sea.
Back cover: One of our island's ethereal views.

Library of Congress Control Number: 2022902234
ISBN: 978-1-66783-151-0

This book was typeset in Interstate, Adobe Garamond Pro, and Winsome.

Printed in the U.S.
2022 2023 2024 / 10 9 8 7 6 5 4 3 2 1

Life on
ORCAS ISLAND

Dedication

I thank you wholeheartedly, Mike, for making our fairytale life here possible, and for encouraging and supporting my creative endeavors along the way. This book exists thanks to your immense gift of time, space, and stability. It is yet *another* dream of mine that you helped support into a reality.

Life on ORCAS ISLAND

BY EDEE KULPER

e
edeeosyncrasies
Eastsound, WA

First Edition

Introduction

Life on Orcas Island is a storybook experience. It is removed, far from the busyness of the mainland—a forested fairytale setting hovering over dark, clear waters.

In its best times, the sun gleams down on stunning natural beauty at every turn, with myriad festivities where not-all-like-minded people gather to hug and laugh and soak in the varied wonder of each other.

In its worst times, clouds blanket the land interminably, and one walks the beaches alone to think, sometimes a little too much.

Either way, an isolated serenity permeates this place. Deep quiet soothes the systems. Loons sing across the Sound, sheep baa in the distance, and newts squiggle under black ponds.

People stop on the street to talk to one another for extended, meaningful conversations. Talents blossom to fill needed niches. Individuality is enjoyed, and conformity is put away. Summer here is bright, warm, and external—a time for jumping off docks into sun-warmed lakes and paddling around sparkling inlets. Winter is dark, rainy, and internal—a time for molding clay and writing plays.

In the following pages, you will see a chronicling of the people, the places, and the experiences that make life here so uncommonly remarkable—a visual time capsule of the past decade, showing who we are and how we do life.

—Edee Kulper

*O*rcas Island may only be ten miles as a crow flies from "America," as locals call it, but it is a world away from the fast life. Time slows down the minute you park in the ferry line to wait for the boat. The fresh air and beautiful scenery bring calm to your systems, and people get out of their cars to shoot the bull until it's time to load. If you're new to these parts, there's an overwhelming feeling of peace and friendliness that pervades the setting.

As soon as everyone boards the ferry, you cross the Salish Sea's Rosario Strait, weaving between densely forested islands. There's even more time to slow down and think, surrounded by ethereal views from every window.

When the ferry arrives at this charming little village scene, you drive off and enter the interior of the island. Beautiful winding roads enshrouded by thick woods open to pastoral scenes dotted with picturesque barns. If you've lived in the city a long time, you find yourself thinking, "I didn't even know places like this still existed."

Orcas Hotel is one of the first things you see when your ferry arrives on the island. For some travelers, it is their respite after a long day's journey of flying, driving, and ferrying. Perched above the water, it is an idyllic place to finally unwind, unpack, and sink into a comfortable chair to watch the last rays of the day's golden light and the comings and goings of illuminated evening ferries as darkness begins to enshroud the land. There's an immediate and deep calm that overtakes you once you're on the island, and a desire to sit and take in the quiet beauty and the clean, fresh air. Visitors have been coming to the Orcas Hotel since its construction in the early 1900s, and it has been everything from a boarding house and a social center with nightly music jams to the location of a proposed ferry lot and eventually a restored building added to the National Register of Historic Places. Chefs John Cox and Julia Felder, who met while working at Big Sur's illustrious Post Ranch Inn, purchased the hotel in February 2020 from Doug and Laura Tidwell, its owners since 1998.

A fifteen-minute drive north from the ferry landing through the agricultural Crow Valley on the west side of the island brings you to the charming town of Eastsound. Looking at a map, you'd think there are several towns dotting the island; those place names are actually little hamlets. Eastsound is the only real town with all the various amenities—stores, banks, shops, schools, churches, and restaurants. It hovers over Fishing Bay, Indian Island, and East Sound, the body of water separating the two sides of the island. Shops and restaurants along the southern side of Main Street face toward the ever-changing coastal scene as mist moves in and out over the water, and the sun's rays take turns beaming majestic brightness through morphing cloud patterns. This opening beside The Madrona Bar and Grill in the heart of town beckons you to walk to the edge of the brick pathway to see what kind of breathtaking scene awaits you on the other side.

This view is from Moran State Park's Mount Constitution, the highest point not only on Orcas Island but in all the San Juan Islands. A stone observation tower at the top of Mount Constitution provides a calm place to decipher which island is which on windy, frigid days. Mount Baker on the mainland even shows its snowy face when the sky is clear. Looking out, you can understand how people living in the San Juan Islands archipelago experience a wide range of lifestyles. Some live in large houses on tiny islands, with boats docked and ready for trips to the mainland to stock up on food and necessities. Others live on islands completely off the grid, generating their own electricity, living minimally, and making do with whatever they can. Some live on sprawling farms or rustic boats while others live in modern condominiums or lavish estates. Blakely Island's roads are small runways, where residents taxi over to their houses. Canoe Island is the site of an internationally-known French Camp. Some islands are protected with state park designations while others are available on real estate sites.

The only way to get to the island is by boat or plane, so it's no wonder that sailors and pilots abound here. It isn't uncommon to run into someone who has sailed around the world and decided to settle on Orcas Island. This is West Sound and its marina.

Perhaps the loveliest quality of this place is the feeling of having time—time to be, time to think, time to pursue your passions, and time to enjoy each other. That isn't to say that everyone is retired. There's just an unhurried feeling in the air. There's no buzz of endless pressure. Here, the air brings deep serenity. Ron Griffin takes time off from landscape construction to relax along the lakeshore with his granddaughter, Phoebe.

This is Buck Bay. Buck Bay Shellfish Farm grows shellfish here, harvesting oysters and digging clams several times a week at low tide to supply its bistro and fish market. They acquire wild-caught fish and other seasonal seafood freshly harvested from the local waters of the Salish Sea by local tribal fishermen. The market, with its flow-through tanks loaded with live oysters, clams, and crabs basking in fresh seawater, allows customers to pick out the shellfish they prefer. A few steps over is the open-air bistro which serves customers a variety of fresh seafood and other dishes inspired by their own organically grown vegetables.

Foragers at heart love picking various seasonal goodies around the island—blackberries, barberries, plums, apples, pears, various greens, mushrooms, and a host of other edibles. Locals like Taryn Kuluris, whose passion is the cultivation and use of nutritional and medicinal plants, take eating to a whole new level. Taryn's artistic, nutrient-dense, from-the-ground dishes involve the creative use of elements like cleavers (sticky weeds), nettles, and rose petals. Above is the fruit of the strawberry tree, not so tasty by the handful unless you have culinary knowledge and skills like Taryn's.

Each island in the San Juans has slightly different topography. You can see the differences when looking at a satellite map. Orcas Island is densely forested, more mountainous (if you could call it that), and has less open farmland. This is a scene from Crow Valley, the interior of the west side of the island, where you'll pass sheep grazing and stands announcing fresh produce and eggs. Drivers can pull over at various stalls, drop money in a receptacle, and bring home colorful salad fixings and a few dozen eggs that were laid that very day.

Beautiful foods, flowers, and botanicals are grown around the island. Fruits, vegetables, and herbs are distributed via CSA memberships (community-supported agriculture), and served in local restaurants and at the Orcas Island Food Bank. OrcaSong Farm, pictured above and at right, is a 130-acre destination botanical farm right in the heart of Crow Valley.

Chance Black and Maura Lynn, both seasoned gardeners, are shown working the land on OrcaSong Farm several years ago. OrcaSong now cultivates and crafts pure, organic botanical products like Organic Lavender Essential Oil, Wildcrafted Red Cedar Hydrosol, and Forest Bath Aromatherapy Refresher. Those are not simply product names that sound nice on store shelves. They encapsulate a bigger story of life among the elements here, as you observe when driving by thousands of lavender plants spreading through OrcaSong's valley. There's something special about buying a fragrant product for your home that was made right on land that you observed, smelled, and experienced. Especially if you only live a few miles away from the very plants it came from.

Orcas Island is shaped like a globby horseshoe, and Eastsound is right in the middle of both sides. It takes about ten minutes to walk its streets, and you can run all your errands within the space of several acres. The population is anywhere from 4,000 to 7,000, depending on the season, and the island is about 57 square miles. Orcas Island has fairly mild seasons, compared to places like Dallas or Chicago. Summer temperatures are in the 70s, fall presents some beautiful colors, and winter temperatures are in the 40s.

Eastsound has all the basics that islanders need, but not a whole lot of overlap. If not for Island Market, Orcas Food Co-op, Ray's Pharmacy, and the various banks in town, we islanders would either have to be much more self-sufficient or that much more reliant on the delivery of mainland goods via the ferry and plane transports of our trusty US Post Office, Aeronautical Services, and FedEx. Shops, restaurants, and various accommodations, from camping and glamping options to charming inns and historic hotels, dot the island. We even have a movie theatre right in Eastsound.

Streets here don't have arbitrary names. Prune Alley is the real deal, where plums fall and disintegrate on the ground. Enchanted Forest Road is thoroughly enchanting. This is Bob Eastman and his wife, Iris. Eastman Road was named for Bob's family. They moved here from Seattle when he was in seventh grade, and Bob went from mowing people's suburban lawns to feeding people's chickens and pigs, bringing in their milk cows, cutting firewood, putting up fences, and digging wells. Bob has fond memories of riding his horse all over Mount Woolard above Eastman Road, and still maintains a love for animals and working outdoors. Bob is about as kind, humble, hard-working, and skilled as they come, and Iris is the ultimate in hospitality when she isn't quilting or sharing in the outdoor chores.

Country roads wind through open meadows and meander through deep forests. But Orcas Island doesn't always look like this. Those same roads in the rainy wintertime influence how we adorn ourselves—in dark colors and rugged shoes—as getting from place to place can become a muddy endeavor. Even walking from the back door to one's car can get pretty messy. We don't exactly look like we've walked out of an LL Bean catalog. Comedian Tim Hawkins has a joke about how people living in the Northwest look like they're always dressed ready for a hike—he's right.

Not only are there chicken eggs, duck eggs, flowers, and produce for sale on the roadsides, there is also firewood, used clothing, and whatever items people want to rehome. This is Black Dog Farm's Thrift Cabin, across from their other cabin with vegetables, books, and dishware for sale.

How fun it is to live in a place where fruit is falling from trees, remnants of old orchards planted in the late 1800s. Around the time that we gleaners are baking our last blackberry cobblers in late summer, branches heavy-laden with fall plums, apples, and pears are begging us to lighten their load.

These happy goats are at Lum Farm on Coffelt Farm Preserve, which is overseen by the ever-knowledgeable, hardworking Eric and Amy Lum. Get marooned on a deserted island in the middle of the sea and hope that those two are on it. If so, you'll not only survive, you'll thrive. For those of us who are "marooned" here with no hands-on experience with raising farm animals, growing food, making cheese, shearing sheep, processing beef—and the list goes on endlessly—it's good to know that the Lums have a lot of important life skills and sell the fruits of their labor at their farm stand.

These pears are for sale on the side of the street in town.

In the quiet, isolated times of the pandemic, Canoe Island French Camp's baker at the time, Alena Harris, began taking orders from other islands for her fantastic chocolate croissants, vegetable galettes, olive and walnut sourdough boules, and more. Executive Director Ben Straub and Camp Director Margaret Schafer delivered the breads and pastries weekly by boat to the camp-owned dock on Orcas Island for pick-up by purchasers.

*D*ays like this are stunning. The air is perfect. The temperature is perfect. There are no mosquitoes, and there are no crowds like the ones you see on the mainland.

But there is a trade-off—the wintertime. It's not the old 'let's-go-shovel-the-snow-off-the driveway-for-the-ninety-ninth-time' kind of winter. In fact, winters are relatively easy here, physically. It's the mental toll that can drive you a little nutty.

Darkness begins to enshroud the land around November. From then on, the thick cloud mass in the sky rarely breaks up to let the sun shine through. Continuous, solid months of gray don't work well with the psyche unless you were raised in the Northwest.

Warm beams of blinding light may finally poke through in March, but sometimes reliably sunshiny days don't happen until July. By August, your whole two-month summer (and newfound glow on sun-kissed skin) begins to dwindle as the kids go back to school and the lake temperatures cool. Fall is beautiful, but sometimes you long for another few months of summer's warmth. It is precisely the perpetual gray "winter" (four to eight months) that keeps the world from clamoring to move here.

It would be fascinating to know how many art studios dot this island, as creativity proliferates here. Mary Jane Elgin, left, is known for her ceramic artistry featured in local galleries. She also teaches classes for adults and children. Sharon Ho, a ceramic and assemblage artist and photographer, hand builds one of her pinch pots above in the Felt+Ceramics Studio|Shop in Eastsound.

Beautiful little enclaves are around every bend. This is Sara's Garden and chapel behind Outlook Inn, named after owner Sara Farish and open daily to the public. Outlook Inn hovers over the bluff in Eastsound, and its fascinating history dates to the late 1800s, when elk herds still roamed the island and lime kiln workers, farmers, occasional trappers, and passing Native Americans populated the region.

Thick snowfall all winter is not the norm, so when we awaken to a white blanket outside our windows, it feels like a magical wonderland. Many residents live along winding dirt roads that traverse various topography and microclimates, so it isn't uncommon for people to be stuck at home until the snow melts. Businesses often close, the power sometimes goes off, and firewood becomes a treasured commodity.

Dan Borman's focus since about 1980 has been finding, growing, and distributing edible, medicinal, and otherwise useful seeds and plants that are proven to grow here, resulting in the Orcas Island Seed Bank, with the help of collaborators Katie Wilkins, Morgan Borman, Marisa Hendron, and others. Many of those seeds are also in the Orcas Island Seed Library, which is inside the public library. Right: Signboards are at every "major" intersection (laughter implied). There are no stoplights on the island, and the maximum speed is 40 miles per hour.

JP and the OK Rhythm Boys—JP Wittman, Gordon Koenig, and Anita Orne—entertain audiences here and throughout the West and have produced three CDs. Their easy use of humor doesn't let on how serious they are about their skill level in a variety of styles and on a variety of instruments. Gordon and Anita have been a couple since the late 1980s, and they collaborate with other musicians including The Olga Symphony, of which Gordon was a founding member in 1983. Their music students have witnessed the thirty-three instruments around their house, from guitars, banjos, mandolins, and accordions to a glockenspiel, theremin, zither, and saws.

Since moving to the island in 1983, Gordon has owned a cookie shop, a flying service, a dress shop, and flown heavy air tankers for the US Forest Service. He handcrafts and sells Barn Swallow Ukuleles made of woods mostly locally sourced from the Northwest. Anita is the music teacher for the Shaw Island School District and the Executive Director of the Orcas Island Chamber Music Festival, which brings world-renowned musicians to the island for their main season in August and throughout the year. While JP doesn't live on Orcas Island, he is a well-known, longtime musical fixture.

Across the water from Eastsound is 1.5-acre Indian Island, which was once used by the Coast Salish people for drying and smoking clams and growing edible camas bulbs. It is open for public access at low tide, when its characteristic tombolo appears, which is a bar of sand that joins the mainland and the island. If you've never seen or heard of a tombolo—many of us hadn't until living here—it's quite a sight. As the tide goes out, a trail that looks strikingly man-made begins to appear under the shallow water. If the tide gets low enough, the slightly elevated bar of sand is no longer covered by water, providing a perfect pathway to Indian Island. But only for a time! Once the tide starts coming in again, water comes in quickly. People exploring the other side of Indian Island may not realize what's happening. It's not uncommon to witness runners rushing to the tombolo, laughing as they realize that a foot or two of water has covered it. Groups of people work out who will carry whom across, and others wade back, shoes and socks in hand.

Canada geese nest on Indian Island, where their loud spring honking can be heard across the Sound. In the warmer months it's common to see research teams of volunteers and schoolchildren working with the Indian Island Marine Health Observatory run by Kwiáht, The Center for the Historical Ecology of the Salish Sea. Russel Barsh, founder and director, and botanist Madrona Murphy, are walking encyclopedias of historical and biological knowledge who continuously study such areas with the aim of preserving them and passing on a sense of stewardship to the next generation.

ur modern global culture tells us that success equates to staying busy, acquiring resources, and keeping up with as much media as possible.

Orcas Island has a very different energy. You feel like you have all the time in the world to think and explore. You slow down and soak in the interactions that come your way. Whether you are a local or a visitor, people make eye contact, say hello to each other, and often value long and meaningful spontaneous conversations when they pass on the street. Drivers wave to one another along the road, even if they don't know each other.

Locals share their gifts with each other, and each new day presents so many workshops, performances, festivities, and gatherings that sometimes you have to intentionally block off a day on your calendar to rest from all the fun. Many of us have meandered through trails leading to the summer Saturday Farmer's Market at the Village Green, or met up at Bill Gincig's free monthly tango, salsa, waltz, and swing classes at the Odd Fellows Hall. We've stopped in at lunchtime to enjoy Emmanuel Episcopal Church's noon Brown Bag Concerts by local musicians. We've packed our calendars with Orcas Island Film Festival dates, Orcas Center performances, and talent shows for kids, adults, and seniors. We've attended Michell Marshall's Woman in the Woods Productions that juxtapose multicultural music and theater with ethnic culinary experiences. We've eaten together at Orcas Christian School's unbelievably generous Chinese, Mexican, and Italian Community Dinners. We've danced in barns and canned seasonal fruit with each other.

Nature is our gallery along the way, and many of us take time to be still and marvel at all the miracles in front of us. Children walk to school through tall-grass fields and densely forested trails. Some even go to school in wilderness "classrooms."

The Emmanuel Episcopal Church with its labyrinth hovering over the Sound is a place where many of us have made memories. We have bowled pumpkins in the grass at fall festivals, eaten ice cream and cookies on 4th of July, bought used items and antiques at their Annual Market Day sale that raises money for church repairs and island nonprofits, attended weddings, and gathered on its ledge to watch the water. These stones and shells were written on and offered by nature crafter and photographer Louise Tucker to passersby on May 1st's World Labyrinth Day.

Many of our kids have grown up taking summer sailing lessons with Sail Orcas, which begin with knowledge classes outside at the Yacht Club and proceed to on-the-water practice in Optis, Bics, and Lasers. Each summer, graduates from the high school sailing team, started in 2001 by Burke Thomas (he coached the team until 2019), return to the island to instruct the four-day camps that span the summer calendar. Kids go from shuddering at the idea of a cold swim test at the start of the week to confidently manning their own craft out in sparkling West Sound. Above is Kai Vurno, taking lessons in his younger years. Kai is now an avid regatta competitor.

Family and women's sailing lessons are also offered. Here, Chris Wolfe is instructing a sold-out women's summer sailing series that Kai's mom, Jen Vurno, far left, is attending. Chris and her husband Justin, the owners of Rainshadow Solar on the island, helped found the Pacific Northwest Shorthanded Sailing Society, won the Pacific Northwest Offshore race up the Washington Coast in the spring of 2021, and represented the US in the 2021 Mixed Offshore Doubles World Championship in Italy, placing sixth after 700 miles of sailing.

MEDLAR
* LET RIPEN TILL SOFT
* LIKE FUDGE WHEN RIPE
$3/BK

Most of us have been on the receiving end of John Steward's relentless work on the land, some of the results of which are shown, opposite. We have relished his delicious gourmet pizzas in spontaneous barn gatherings and at Hogstone's Wood Oven, and we have enjoyed his beautiful and varied produce from Maple Rock Farm, which supplied residents, restaurants, and the Orcas Island Food Bank with environmentally-minded fruits and vegetables through the years.

Chama Anderson, beloved founder of the Orcas Lady Vikings Soccer Team, has a quality unlike many people you come across on this earth. Even after experiencing a tragic accident that changed her life, words can't adequately explain the feeling of groundedness, balance, and depth that she exudes. Chama embodies what you imagine when you think of an old soul. There is an unspoken yet inherent quality of spirituality and love that emanates from within her.

Meet Ricky the bearded dragon, owned by the Neal family and crowned the Honorary Mayor of Orcas Island on July 4, 2021. Any animal can run for mayor—a dog, cat, bunny, donkey, whale, you name it—thanks to this creative fundraiser that benefits Orcas Island Children's House, an infant-toddler center and preschool. Mayoral candidates campaign for votes that people can buy for $1 apiece. Final votes often cast by enthusiastic children cascade in after the 4th of July parade, where people gather at the Village Green to meet and pet the candidates. Ricky's final tally was a whopping 19,824 votes, beating the other six candidates including closest competitor, canine Stanley Tucci, who received 17,724 votes.

Orcas Islanders have celebrated 4th of July in various ways over the years, as you will see on the following pages. Mount Baker Farm's train takes passengers on its 1.2-mile track complete with two stations built by previous owner and railway enthusiast, Burton Burton. Train rides and live music entertain locals gathered in and around their cars, preparing for an evening 4th of July Laser Light Show, shown on the next page. Notice the faint glimpse of fading evening light on Mount Baker in the background.

An annual hallmark of 4th of July is Matthew Laslo's Magic Show at Sea View Theatre. Islanders have had the joy of watching Matthew the Magician hone his phenomenal skills onstage since he was 13 years old. Above is the Harvey Family Logging Show at the Village Green, a tradition since the 1980s. At left is the 4th of July Laser Light Show entertaining about 600 onlookers in and around their cars at Mount Baker Farm.

It isn't every day that you watch fireworks shooting off a barge over the water. That has been the norm here for many years after enjoying the other 4th of July festivities—Deer Harbor fireworks on July 3rd, the Annual 5K and kids' 1K in Eastsound on the morning of the 4th, the pancake breakfast and salmon barbecue at the fire station, the parade through town, and the farmers' market and pie booth at the Village Green. Uncharacteristic droves of people gaily fill the streets and gather in the grass above Eastsound Beach to enjoy live patriotic music at dusk by the Community Band, ice cream sundaes at the Emmanuel Episcopal Church, and fireworks over Fishing Bay.

Lakes and ponds are common features on the island. Islanders and visitors swim in them, net tadpoles the size of their palms in them, gather buckets of newts along their edges, attend weddings and baptisms on their shores, and slide across their frozen surfaces in the winter.

This pond is on the property of the practice of Dr. Vincent Shu, a cardiologist and acupuncturist who graduated from medical school in Taiwan in 1977 and specializes in the integration of Eastern and Western medicine techniques. Dr. Shu picks up where Western medicine and invasive technologies leave off, addressing ailments with long-practiced techniques that are shockingly gentle and often extraordinarily effective.

Since 2001, Mike O'Connell has managed the Glenwood Springs Hatchery, which releases over 750,000 juvenile Chinook salmon each year. It all began as an experiment in 1978 by Long Live the Kings founder Jim Youngren, whose aim was restoring wild salmon and steelhead populations. Several times a year, community members don their chest waders and converge in the collection pool below the hatchery stream to collect fish for their roe and milt (eggs and sperm) as groups of local schoolchildren help with the work and scientists collect data. Mike's son, Soren, has grown up following in his dad's footsteps; here, he's working alongside Rick Doty.

Neighborhoods aren't typical grids of streets. Houses might be close by or separated by dozens or even hundreds of acres, distinct from each other due to the land's differing physical features in between. One neighbor may have flat, sunny property great for farming while another is perched on a rocky cliff promontory above the sea, surrounded by deep, dark forest.

Joanie Rorabaugh, originally from Cape Elizabeth, Maine, knew she wanted to own a kayak store the first time she ever got in a kayak. She opened Crescent Beach Kayak Rentals in 1993 beside her now-shimmering, goldish-green residence, and has since displayed various wooden carvings around the property that reflect her different moods. You can't mistake her positivity, ever-bright smile, and always-colorful attire. Her current medium of choice is large-scale, fused-glass sculpture. She shares her life with David Johnson, a man of endless interests and passions. Opposite: Low tide reveals the stunning marine life surrounding us. Children love darting between water-spouting geoducks (pronounced "gooey" ducks) and turning over rocks to find dozens of fast-moving crabs. Every now and then, a clump of squid egg capsules is revealed, and in some places live sand dollars cover the shallow sea floor.

Driftwood thickly lines Crescent Beach's shore, providing ample material for creative construction. It is common to walk along the beach and come upon driftwood structures decorated with branches and shells, words written in sticks and stones, and sometimes even mini-monuments big enough for small gatherings, such as this. It all changes by the day and the tides.

If you go out and look around during a rare freeze, you'll see extraordinary views few people see of this place. Crescent Beach looks almost polar here—a fleeting sight soon changed by warming temperatures, as weather here can flip in an instant.

Midnight sights like this are not common. This was an unusual night of building chaotic winds and snow flurries blasting left and right. No one was out. Streets were barren. There was no activity anywhere except for the lone, wild torrent of air and moisture blasting at anything in its way. The calming, yellow-orange light emanating from Emmanuel Episcopal Church's windows beamed out in stark contrast to the cold, dark frenzy outside. Its gentle warmth was mesmerizingly peaceful, undaunted by the relentless winter tyrant pounding on the outside walls of the church.

On the same night, Orcas Island Community Church's parking lot was covered in a thick mantle of snow like smooth, white fondant—something that would neither last long with changing island temperatures nor remain untouched by playful children in the morning. A shaft of light above the steeple lit every manic, flitting snowflake in its path, making a concentrated light show of movement reaching up into the sky above. Both churches were quietly replying to the elements, "The light shines in the darkness, and the darkness has not overcome it." (JOHN 1:5)

There are several places on the island where gargantuan icicles form when the temperature gets low enough. Again, sights like this are rare and fleeting, as the tide will soon rise to melt the Goliath-sized behemoths that formed one trickle at a time, seeping out of the rock during the night like instant stalactites.

Snow signals an almost instant closure of the road leading up to our island's highest point, Mount Constitution. When that happens, the only way to get there is by foot. It's quite an experience. You begin at an elevation where rain is soaking the road, but as you gradually wind up one step at a time, the consistency of the moisture changes until you're standing knee-deep in white powder. The road morphs into a magical white fairytale unlike anything that lower-elevation residents usually see. This is a 3:40 p.m. late December view from the top of the observation tower, looking toward Sucia and Matia Islands, less than an hour before nightfall.

Darvill's Bookstore is one of our most cozy, cherished shops on the island, owned and operated since 1975 by Jenny Pederson. Pictured are just two of the books written by local San Juan Island biologist and speaker, Thor Hanson. Take a look at four of his titles to get an idea of the fascinating kind of work he is pursuing on a daily basis here in our island community:

Hurricane Lizards and Plastic Squid: The Fraught and Fascinating Biology of Climate Change (2021)

Buzz: The Nature and Necessity of Bees (2019)

The Triumph of Seeds: How Grains, Nuts, Kernels, Pulses, & Pips Conquered the Plant Kingdom and Shaped Human History (2015)

Feathers: The Evolution of a Natural Miracle (2012)

Jenny's mother, Catherine Pederson, a beloved local piano instructor, welcomes store visitors during the Christmas holiday. A snowy scene in the heart of Eastsound mirrors the magical feel of the Best-in-Show winning creation by Bonnie Mahony at the first annual Gingerbread Contest put on by the Funhouse and Island Market. All lights are turned off at Orcas Island Community Church's Candlelight Christmas Eve service, then one candle is lit and its light is spread from person to person until the sanctuary is glowing.

The gift Orcas Island always provides is the time and space to sit in a peaceful place and ponder life. Or notice a tiny scene in a colorful planter in town or in a faraway meadow that will only last for a day, a week, or a month before it disappears until next year. It is in these moments of stillness and contemplation that we often have life-shifting thoughts that propel us into new ways of living and relating, or reorient us toward goals or adventures in ways we may not have dreamed up in busy moments. The beauty and quiet of Orcas Island reminds us to be, observe, and breathe.

Camp Orkila is a 280-acre YMCA property on the island's northwest shore that has welcomed children and families from all over the country and the world to its camps since 1906. Camp Orkila also generously hosts local events. Here, racers "run" through a knee-deep channel of water at the start of the Spring ROAR—a rogue obstacle adventure race. Alyson Stephens, our ever-upbeat resident Zumba instructor, at left, is always game for an active challenge with a smile on her face. Alyson and her husband Andrew are both physical therapists at her husband's practice, Orcas Island Physical Therapy, along with fellow physical therapist and co-owner, Scott Heisinger.

Leon Sommé and Shawna Franklin met in a kayak rolling class in college and have been together ever since. They co-founded the world-renowned paddle boards school Body Boat Blade International in Eastsound. Now retired from being coaches and coach educators, you'll see them holding hands while walking around the upper deck of the ferry, or pursuing all of the other aspects of living on Orcas Island that they didn't have time for before, from mountain biking and hiking to windsurfing and down-winding on stand-up paddleboards. They love doing everything together. Shawna is also a full-time artist working out of her home studio, and her work is featured in Crow Valley Gallery and Orcas Island Artworks. Artworks, above, is a cooperative gallery in Olga displaying varied work from dozens of local artists and craftspeople, and Shawna's work has been featured there since 1996.

Father Berto Gándara-Perea of Emmanuel Episcopal Church is joy incarnate. His warm energy and welcoming presence invite meaningful conversation and an undeniable sense of belonging. Here, he is marrying Church Secretary Lisa Heisinger's mother, Beth Lorenzen, and Ed Walter. Before coming to Orcas Island in 2014, Fr. Berto served in the Dominican Republic, Belgium, Spain, Puerto Rico, and Harlem. He speaks English, Spanish, and French, and is a native of Puerto Rico. Opposite: Every time you are invited to experience an event at Emmanuel Episcopal Church—whether it be a wedding, a workshop, a holiday celebration, or a concert—you feel overwhelmingly fortunate to get to make memories in the unparalleled beauty of its setting, whether the sun is shining down or a looming storm darkens the skies and churns up the waters below. Either way, there is a powerful beauty that gives you a sense of grateful awe for getting to experience it.

The Annual Artists' Studio Tour is one of the wonderful events that makes Orcas Island so unique. Not only is it free, you are welcomed onto people's properties to tour their studios as artists of all kinds give live demonstrations of their work. You are given a map, and you have three days to stop at as many studios as you'd like between certain hours.

Michael Yeaman's background in geology and geophysics informs his passion for stone sculpture. He built the monument above to commemorate his thirtieth wedding anniversary with his wife, Debra Nichols.

The work of Orcas-born and raised, second-generation blacksmith and sculptor, Zackarya Leck, is in public spaces and private collections around the island and beyond. He is deeply inspired by the ocean, as seen in his seventy-foot forged Corten Steel *Kelp Forest* at the ferry terminal. Zackarya helped build the nature-based play area in Eastsound's Village Green in collaboration with Chuck Greening and Mark Mayer, and above, he works on one of a series of commissioned prawns.

Drive into a gated area leading to a plane-hangar neighborhood on our island's tiny airstrip, and you've arrived at Kim Middleton's studio, top right. Kim's dazzlingly colorful paintings of birds convey her love and knowledge of the avian world. Kim has also led birding tours around the world.

Genuine, lighthearted Barbara Gourley, middle, exudes positivity when she explains her art in her warm, bright studio that doubles as a guesthouse.

Kandis Susol, right, explains how she tries to affect negative situations with positive change through her encaustic paper sculptures. Her large pieces take at least 300 hours each, one of which was made after she watched Ai Wei Wei's *Human Flow* documentary about refugees.

We all know Ronni Silva as the beaming face of road work. Whenever you pass the yellow-orange San Juan County Public Works Department trucks and tractors, she is there with a big smile. Whether she's working in mud and pouring rain with fellow equipment operators or directing traffic around flooded roads, she always has time for a calm, kind exchange.

Uzek Susol has built a business as an honest, meticulous mechanic since 1990, and is adept at rescuing people needing a tow in all kinds of hazardous conditions. He is exactly the kind of person you'd want help from in a hard time—kind-hearted, grounded, and calm under pressure.

Kristy Bredin decided to set aside her New York City life and pursue a path as an herbalist in 2009. She moved to the San Juan Islands and has since worked alongside Ryan Drum, a retired botany professor, herbal medicine expert, and specialist in wildcrafting herbs, local plants, and seaweeds. Kristy continues Ryan's work by teaching locally and worldwide about wild plant medicines and seaweeds, and by wildcrafting herbs that she sells through her company, Mermaid Botanicals. She is continuously working with elements from the soil, land, and sea, and here she collects hawthorn berries known for helping digestion and heart functions.

Islanders gather at the entrance of protected Native land at the end of Haven Road in Eastsound to support and send off members of the Lummi Nation who organized a two-week, cross-country journey to Washington, D.C., to raise awareness for the protection of sacred tribal lands while hauling a newly-carved 5,000-pound totem pole. Stops along the "Red Road to D.C.," as it was called, included speeches by master carver Jewell Praying Wolf James (his name is Se-Sealth in the Lummi language), shown above, until the ultimate destination was reached—the front entrance of the National Museum of the American Indian in the National Mall.

Orcas Island Library is one of the largest and highest-elevation structures in town and is a big part of many residents' lives. Phil Heikkinen, the director for seventeen years (now retired), plays chess with Max Vollmer, Chase Connell, and Elijah Griffith on the outskirts of the gigantic parking lot book sale at the Annual Library Fair. The library's Annual Holiday Tea in December is a cherished gathering. The Friends of the Library organize the baking of hundreds of goodies, the appearance of Santa and Mrs. Claus, and musical entertainment by fun-loving talents such as Marj Franke and Carl Burger, above. Opposite: The library grounds, which overlook the not-too-distant Sound, provide a lush setting for reading and contemplation.

Mindy Sonshine and Mike Connell elevated an avocation into a full-time, exceedingly professional business when they opened Orcas Island Leather Goods in April 2021. From the leather products they make and the feel of the environment they've created in their store to the photography and advertising they've posted online, every aspect of their business is thoughtfully planned and executed, and top notch. It's impressive to see what this couple—once professional photographers and founders of a photography editing company—has dreamed up and made into reality.

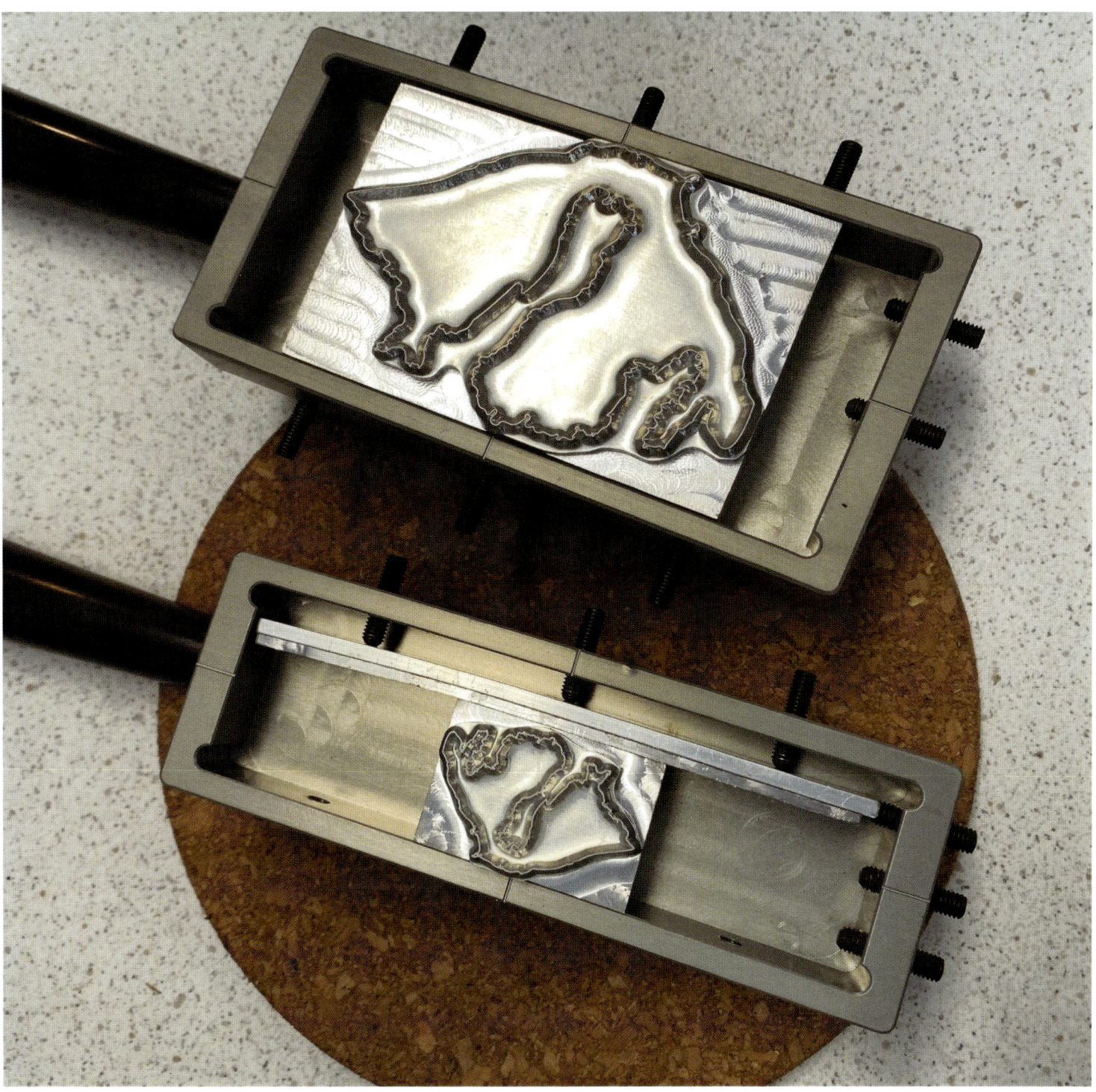

Chris and Eliza Morris began their Island Thyme business of botanically-based skin and body products in 1996. They grow many of the ingredients they use right on their farm here, and their exceptional natural creams, balms, and oils are dazzling eye candy on the shelves of their beautiful Eastsound store. As a side note, "island time" is a very real feeling here—a relaxed take on schedules and punctuality (not at all indicative of the Morrises' work ethic).

Audra Lawlor stops for a moment amid bubbling copper cauldrons of what will soon be Cherry Fig Leaf Spoon Preserves, surrounded by son Life, daughter Neve, and thriving business Girl Meets Dirt. Eschewing the steel and concrete of Wall Street for fresh air and orchards, she's built a life around the fruits of the land, creating various spoon preserves, cutting preserves, bitters, and heirloom fruit syrups called shrubs, far right.

Island Thyme
Sandalwood
Citrus Soap

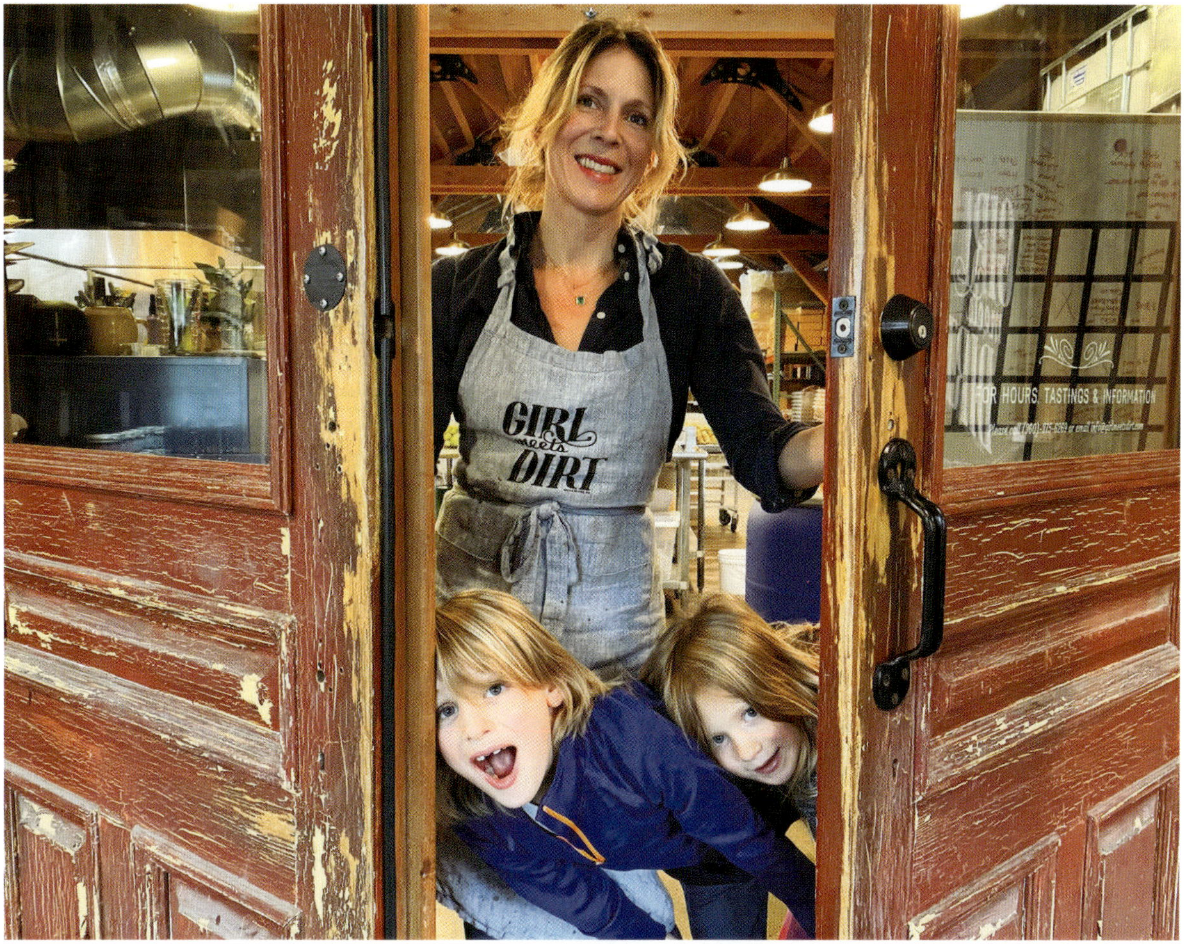
GIRL
meets
DIRT
FOR HOURS, TASTINGS & INFORMATION

SHRUB
GIRL
meets
DIRT

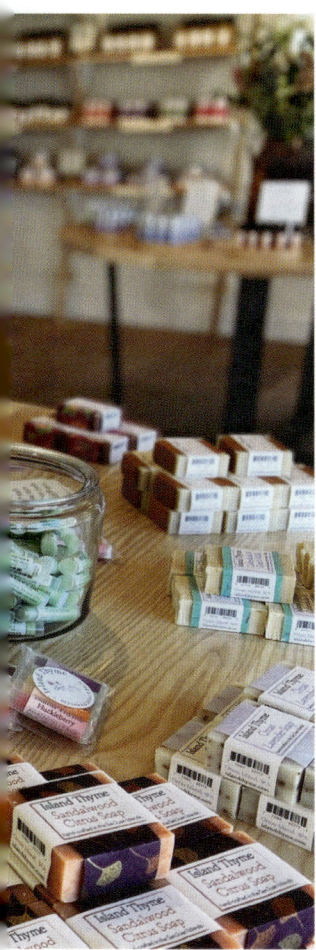

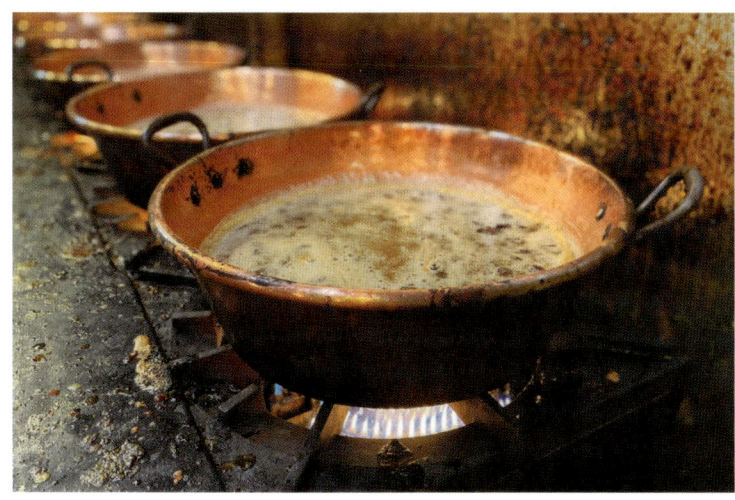

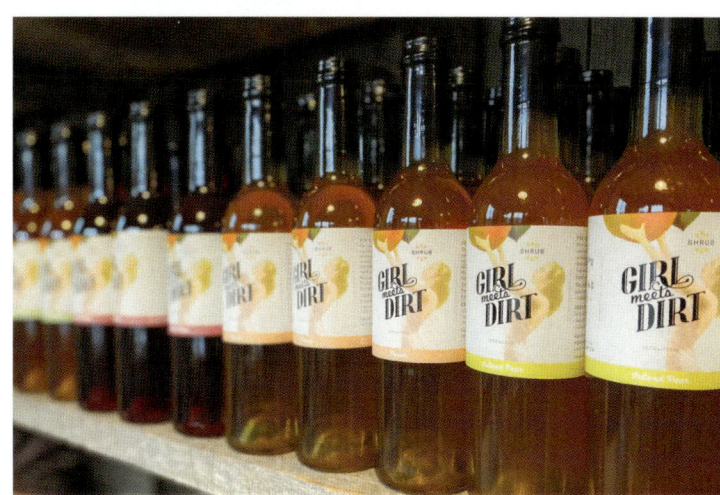

Paul Freedman began teaching in 1992 and founded Salmonberry School in 2001 as a holistic alternative to standard educational institutions. Here, he helps Lael Watson in the process of carving a spoon from a piece of wood while on a class day trip in Moran State Park. Eve Eon, right, prepares to do some journaling in a chosen wilderness spot. Paul taught in (and outside of) the classroom for twenty-eight years, and transitioned to Head of Salmonberry School after the 2020–2021 school year. Many people on the island have memories of Salmonberry's various and sundry summer camps, such as Chickens 101, Medieval Camp, Pioneer Camp, Spanish Camp, Parkour Camp, and more.

Salmonberry has often collaborated with Cody Beebe, of Earthways Nature Education, whose specialty is teaching kids wilderness survival skills such as navigation, tracking, tool making, and shelter building. Above, Leah Jenson uses techniques Cody has taught her to burn a divot for her spoon with a hot coal from the fire.

The performing arts are a big deal here. Clockwise from top: Lili Pritchard as Tybalt and Ash Gordon as Lady Capulet rehearsing for Orcas Christian School's production of Romeo and Juliet, directed by ever-exuberant English and history teacher Andy Rivera. This was Orcas Center's costume room under Deborah Sparks' supervision. Sparks was the Theatre Productions Director from 2001–2017, doing everything from costume, lighting, and set design to producing, directing, and acting in plays and musicals. Tiffany Loney's and Aristotle Luna's boys' dance class performing at Orcas Center. Rachel Lum, an aerial silks acrobat at a summer concert finale at the Village Green. Tiffany Loney's "Shooting Stars" performing on 4th of July at the Village Green.

Syd Exton, third generation potter and owner of Orcas Island Pottery, beams next to fellow potter and son, Aaron Hardy. Two of her other children, Matt Haeuser and Kimberly Hardy, are also potters whose creations grace the indoor shelves and characteristic summer outdoor tables. Syd threw her first pot at the age of five, as knowledge was passed down from her mother and grandmother. She became the manager and lead potter of Orcas Island Pottery in 1989 and inherited the place in 1993. Opposite is the property's magnificent treehouse that was built around a 200-year-old cedar.

Madrona trees dot the island, with dark yellow skin that feels oddly human-like and rich orange bark that jumps out against bright blue summer skies. They are often the muse of local artists, which you will see in painter James Hardman's work while perusing Orcas Island Artworks in Olga.

There are workshops galore, taught by musicians, gardeners, scientists, beekeepers, artists, tech-lovers, you name it. This is Lopez Island botanist and genetic technician Madrona Murphy, of Kwiáht, teaching apple grafting at the Orcas Island Historical Museum as homeschooler Colt Johnson learns her techniques. Many attendees of this workshop may now have trees mature enough to support three or four fruiting varieties each fall.

Thanks to the San Juan County Land Bank conserving exceptional areas around the islands, residents can hike to stunning vistas like this. Opposite: We cohabitate with lichen, moss, mud, and mold, thanks to months and months of dripping skies. It isn't a pretty result inside a home at times but all that dampness makes a wonderland of growth outside. Winter hiking promises vignettes of endless undulating mossy rocks and beautiful specimens of colorful lichen.

Now and then we witness stunning marine life. It's a rare sight to see a giant Pacific octopus washed up on the beach, or to recognize that a clear but camouflaged hooded nudibranch is "swimming" by you in the water.

Joe Gaydos, chief scientist at The SeaDoc Society overlooking West Sound, works not only as a marine researcher on land and under the water, he and the SeaDoc team work to educate the public on making wise decisions that affect the environment and the species all around us, from the critically endangered Southern Resident killer whales to the Chinook salmon they eat. Gaydos co-authored the book at left with Audrey DeLella Benedict, shown in the window of our local bookstore, in order to inspire and educate the younger generations to be good future stewards of the Salish Sea. The SeaDoc Society has also been known to pack Sea View Theatre with their "Ocean Nights" film and lecture series.

Karl Krüger began cross-country skiing when he learned to walk, climbed his first high Adirondack peak at 3, climbed the rest by age 11, taught himself to windsurf at 12, and became a sailing instructor at 17. He has been a ski and snowboard racer, a rock, ice, and alpine climbing guide, and in 2017, he became the first person to paddle the 750-mile Race to Alaska course on a standup paddle board. In August 2022, he plans to be the first person to navigate 1,900 miles of the Northwest Passage on a paddle board. This is his custom-made board, Raven, built exactly to his specifications. No board like this exists in the world.

Leo Lambiel spent over fifty years collecting thousands of art pieces from mostly local artists, turning his house into an ever-expanding gallery and giving fascinating two-hour tours of the property inside and out. A perfectionist woodworker and artist himself, evident in his Greek temple replica at left, he transformed his 24 x 24-foot cabin into a stunning manor over the years. These photos were taken on his last tour. His passion came to an abrupt end due to a confluence of difficult circumstances, and his dream of passing his giant art collection over to a community college didn't get to happen. Nevertheless, Leo was a master at transforming all of his other larger-than-life aspirations into phenomenal artistic realities.

Eastsound, opposite, hovers over the ever-changing Sound. Kids grow up here immersed in nature, from incubating duck eggs and raising chickens to exploring low-tide biomes full of marine treasures like tiny midshipman fish still attached to rocks and red sea cucumbers in tide pools. Canada geese announce their courtship on Indian Island, where open-air goose nests hold precious eggs.

Camp Orkila's Annual Fall Festival is an outdoor gathering that families look forward to every year, complete with zip lining, archery, hayrides, wall climbing, donut-dangling, goat petting, and pumpkin painting. The staff at this oh-so-generous event works hard to cook and serve what seem like endless pots of homemade soup and gallons upon gallons of fresh-pressed apple cider made from apples harvested from the property. Families come back at night for the renowned tractor-driven haunted hayride.

Brett McFarland pushes wife and fellow teacher Jill Sherman out from the shore of Crescent Beach into Ship Bay during a favorite Halloween morning tradition called Witches on the Water, begun by local massage therapist and doula, Erin Wild. This "Ruth" skin-on-frame performance wherry was built by Brett's physics class at Orcas Island High School. They fabricated all the parts based on detailed plans designed by Dave Gentry. Brett teaches his students through hands-on projects, building chairs, bikes, boats, sheds, and tiny homes.

One of the many unique events that makes this place special is Young Eagles Day. (Not to be confused with the Annual Orcas Island Fly-In the first weekend in August.) One day each June, experienced local pilots volunteer their time and their planes to give 25-minute rides to children from 8 to 17 years old. Pilot Beverly Franklet, above, told her mother at age 10 that she wanted to become the youngest licensed female pilot in the country. Beverly became a pilot in 1992 when only six percent of pilots were female. She volunteered on Young Eagles Day for over 15 years and flew 130 kids. Dr. David Shinstrom, opposite, a family doctor for nearly three decades (now retired), flies Milana Schneider and his canine companion, Paqo, who accompanies him on all of his flights. Teenagers and adults who want to take their skills to the next level can enroll in the Airhawks Flying Club to obtain their private pilot's license. At least three kids who flew with Dr. Shinstrom went on to get their pilot's licenses, and one joined the Air Force. The plane hangar, below, is like a museum in the making, its walls covered with paraphernalia from the pilots who have enjoyed this space together over the years.

Dense forested hikes open to some of the most breathtaking precipices you can ever imagine, while tiny little miracles along the trails can be completely overlooked underfoot.

Colleen Stewart, left, has been the Farm to Classroom Gardener and Coordinator since 2015 at the public school's educational garden. Over the years she has cultivated a diverse array of perennial, annual, culinary, native, medicinal, dye, textile, fruiting, vining, carnivorous, and ornamental plants alongside students in grades K–8, and fellow educators Mandy Randolph and Jennifer Pietsch. Students enjoy garden-related activities and projects each week throughout the school year.

Chelsea Thorpe, above, cuts samples of apple and pear varieties at Warm Valley Farm for visitors on the Annual Farm Tour that happens in October. The owners of the farm are Greenpeace ship Captain Joel Stewart (unrelated to Colleen) and singer and building designer Annie McIntyre. Both farms have been stops on the weekend-long tour, a self-guided event that provides maps for visitors to observe various established, thriving farms around the island.

Since 1860, Olga has been one of the island's small community hamlets, named after the mother of its first storekeeper, Anthony Ohlert. The Olga Store across from the dock has been a community hub for islanders on the east side since 1937 and was purchased in 2020 by community nonprofit Friends of the Olga Store Building, thanks to hundreds of donations. Once renovated, the store will house the Olga Post Office and an extension of the Orcas Food Co-op, and will provide essential services and community space.

Dave Baxter, left, of Lieber Haven Resort, which overlooks Obstruction Pass Bay, remembers every last detail of his life from a young age. At 6, he acted as translator on phone conversations between his deaf father (a freelance political strategist) and President Roosevelt. Nixon was a common guest in his living room. In his young years he was on his way to becoming a concert pianist. At the age of 8, he began building a house, and by 15 he had built two homes and a cottage in California. He went on to become a sought-after woodworker and boatbuilder to the rich and famous after an internship at the age of 18. *He* needs to write a book.

Mandy Troxel, top left, is a farm manager, felt-worker, singer, songwriter, and folk musician. In 2014, she produced a full-length album on her independent label, Arooo Music. In 2020, she created and maintained a wonderful music blog for kids, part of a program that was sponsored by the Orcas Island Chamber Music Festival. She also performs with a trio called Raising Hazel.

A segment of painter Stephanie Iverson's 13 x 80-foot marine mural in Eastsound, as featured on the cover of our local newspaper, *The Islands' Sounder*. The *Sounder* and *theOrcasonian* online are our primary local news sources.

The funky and beloved drop-off-your-unwanteds and name-your-price-for-used-stuff Exchange, founded by George Post and other volunteers in 1981, burned down in 2013 and reopened in a beautiful, more functional structure in November 2017. Manager Jeff Ludwig, smiling above, and Executive Director Pete Moe of the adjoining Orcas Recycling Services are the faces of these important institutions.

Elizabeth Schermerhorn, owner of clothing store Faraways Boutique, is conducting one of her evening "lives," selling merchandise to viewers tuning in online.

The Annual Children's Christmas Market at the library is so very special. Any child can enter, and dozens of local kids spend weeks preparing handmade wares to sell for under $10 each. It's wonderful to see what kinds of creations the kids dream up each year. This is Nootka Townsend, who's been selling out of her varying wares of hand-drawn prayer flags, origami twinkle-light decorations, and painted chopsticks every year since she was tiny. Laura Ludwig and Stephanie Iverson, Nootka's mother, revel in the festivities.

It's been a tradition to walk through the warm, cozy atmosphere of the Annual Holiday Artisan's Faire at the Odd Fellows Hall and marvel at Susie Shipman's Island Bound Books, Christina Orchid's Red Rabbit Farm jams, Kyle Jepsen and Cari Darner's HOLeY CAN! tin can lanterns, Jessie Morrow's Material Wit jewelry, Carla Stanley's illustrations about Orcas Island on paper goods, Black Dog Farm's one-of-a-kind potted narcissus plants, and Bossy's Feltworks' needle-felted animal creations, just to name a few vendors. Maria Bullock grows and weaves different varieties of willow at her home, Bullock's Permaculture Homestead, where for decades her husband Douglas and his brothers Joe and Sam have taught world-renowned workshops. These works of functional art for sale at the Artisan's Faire, right, are some of Maria's many creations. She also teaches European basketry, is the founder of Island Aerial Acrobatics, and is Matthew the Magician's on-stage magic assistant.

Santa comes to Deer Harbor by boat every December and is then driven over to the Deer Harbor Community Club, above, where children meet him to sit on his lap, choose a present from an overflowing table of amazingness, and eat beautiful cookies. It's a sweet, generous event in the memories of most children growing up here, thanks to the Deer Harbor Women's Auxiliary. A Santa Ship also comes to the ferry landing each year, thanks to the Lions Club, where there are festivities for families right on the dock.

Wildlife surrounds us. Eagles soar and screech in the sky above. Kingfishers skim the water's surface. Wild rabbits graze in meadows, and collared dove fledglings try not to get eaten on the ground before they can fly. Mink terrorize fenced-in domesticated ducks. And gentle deer are all over the place. This is called a piebald deer because it's lacking pigment in some areas. Opposite: Typical nature findings you'll stumble upon here—antlers, skulls, oyster shells, beach stones, and horse chestnuts. (Don't eat them; they're toxic.)

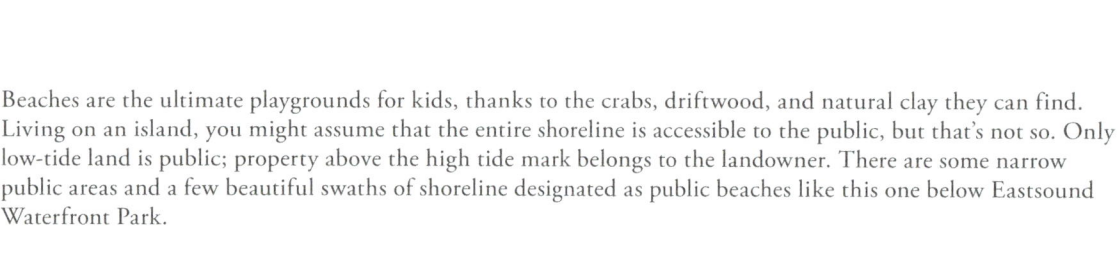

Beaches are the ultimate playgrounds for kids, thanks to the crabs, driftwood, and natural clay they can find. Living on an island, you might assume that the entire shoreline is accessible to the public, but that's not so. Only low-tide land is public; property above the high tide mark belongs to the landowner. There are some narrow public areas and a few beautiful swaths of shoreline designated as public beaches like this one below Eastsound Waterfront Park.

Kathy Morris, opposite, runs West Beach Farm with her family and often shears sheep for onlookers in the Annual Orcas Island Farm Tour. Her family raises grass-fed beef and lamb, and pastured pork. West Beach Farm runs one of the many farm stands on the island, with abundant fresh vegetables, eggs, meats, and Endswell Bakehouse bread handmade by Heather Immoor. Heather's toasted sesame sourdough is some of the best bread you'll ever taste. Many island farm stands are unmanned and operate on the honor system.

Halloween is extra special on our island, where there aren't typical suburban neighborhoods for trick-or-treating. The shops of Eastsound host the evening, closing North Beach Road to traffic so that costumed children can take over the street and go from shop to shop collecting candy. Adults join in the fun too. This is Melanie Flint, granddaughter of longtime residents Velma and Richard Doty, in the courtyard beside the Orcas Food Co-op. In 1971, the Dotys purchased the A-1 food shack that was here and built new structures to make it Doty's A-1 Café and Bakery, and their home until 2001. Melanie, a nanny and aspiring teacher, grew up with a love for *Mary Poppins* and anything with Julie Andrews, and often dreamt of reenacting scenes from her favorite films right above this courtyard. Many eating establishments have been and are second homes to the family members looking after them, such as the Carpenters of Deer Harbor Inn, the Rios family of Mijitas, and the Bledsoes of the original Teezer's.

The Orcas Island Vikings Co-ed Soccer Team, coached by Terry Turner, returns to the island from an early November Sunday morning ferry after winning the 2021 State Championship. Families and fans gather to cheer them on as they pass through town.

Shipbuilder and former Seattle Mayor Robert Moran, born in 1857, was warned by physicians in 1904, at the age of 47, that his stress level was so high after building the battleship USS *Nebraska* that he might only have six months to live. He responded by retiring to Orcas Island in 1906, acquiring 7,800 acres, and building the formidable mansion that is the focal point of Rosario Resort today. He ended up living forty more years to the age of 86. General manager, resident historian, and pianist Christopher Peacock has entertained visitors for over thirty years with weekly piano and organ concerts in the resort's stunning Music Room.

Rosario Resort is on the east side of the island and hovers above the water on a promontory that rests about halfway up East Sound, facing south. To the right is the Sound, which continues past the resort toward the town of Eastsound. To the left is Cascade Bay with a marina that welcomes guests who have arrived by boat. Thanks to Moran's donation of 2,700 acres to the state to be set aside as a park in 1921 (he donated more land later), we all enjoy the beautiful Moran State Park, now over 5,400 acres to the east (if you were to look left from this spot).

Riding the ferry is a part of life in the San Juan Islands. Without the ferry system, we would be much more isolated. Ferries run all day, transporting riders between the islands of Orcas, San Juan, Lopez, and Shaw, and to and from the mainland terminal in Anacortes. People living on the smaller islands must coordinate their own transportation, whether by mail boat or personal craft. The cost of taking the ferry is close to $50 for a standard car and its driver, and an adult passenger costs about $15. Inter-island walk-ons are free. Above, the sun sets in the channel between Shaw and Orcas Islands.

Clear-day views from the ferry are breathtaking. Fierce, windy days make you thankful to be inside the warm upper deck, calmly piecing together jigsaw puzzles on the tables. Ferries run even in storms and rough seas, and waves have been known to smash through the windshields of vehicles in the front row of the car deck, though that's extremely rare. A calm morning dawns, above, as the ferry stops at Lopez Island on its way to the mainland.

Kaj and Tashi Litch, the phenomenal young musical brothers known as Brograss, are performing onstage at the Village Green as their mother, local violin instructor Rachel Bishop, sells merchandise to the crowd. We've watched Kaj and Tashi playing music with their parents as Crow Valley String Band since they were in grade school (their father, Jim Litch, plays bass in the band). Other talented performers locals have watched grow up onstage are the aforementioned Matthew the Magician, singer and actress Stormy Hildreth, dancer Aristotle Luna, and the trio Almost Classical—violinist Emy Carter, pianist Lisa Carter, and violinist Paris Wilson.

Composer, arranger, and musician Martin Lund, right, is fluent in and ever-joyously comfortable playing the piano, clarinet, saxophone, flute, and accordion. He has been involved in jazz, Broadway, rock, and classical productions near and far and has instructed some of our best young talents.

There have been ongoing shifts to our health institutions on the island, and these beloved, unflagging family doctors—David Russell, Camille Fleming, and Michael Alperin—worked together to care seamlessly for us through the changes. Islanders are also faithfully served by dozens of Fire Department staff and volunteers. Most of us have yearly memberships to Airlift Northwest and Island Air Ambulance, services that can speedily evacuate residents off the island via helicopter or plane to the nearest hospital on the mainland.

Graduates from Orcas Island High School drive a circuit through town as residents come out on the streets to cheer them on. Middle School and High School Principal Kyle Freeman and Elementary School Principal Lorena Stanvekich (in the fire truck) wave to Jaydon Krisch Derr, headed for the US Naval Academy.

It's been an annual tradition for Orcas Island High School seniors to paint the barn across from Fowler's Pond Preserve on Orcas Road. The dilapidating barn was finally retired after its adornment by the class of 2014 (though a future class tried to keep it going). Former Councilman Rick Hughes and Ray's Pharmacy owner Marlace Hughes own the property and built a new barn, ripe for future coats of paint.

Power outages are part of life here, where high winds and storms can cause unforeseen damage to lines supplying power to several neighborhoods or entire islands. Businesses and schools close, people can't work, and there's no telling how long an outage will last. Life reverts to the simpler days of candles, books, and family time by the fireplace. This is downtown Eastsound during an outage at night. The only light is coming from Island Market, whose severe food losses during past outages encouraged them to invest in a generator since the community depends on them as the major food source. Their ability to retain power now saves the rest of us when we need warm food and supplies.

In November 2021, a voluminous multi-day downpour caused destructive flooding around the island and a complete wash-out of Point Lawrence Road just beyond Doe Bay Resort. Residents were stranded on the far east side of the island, but quick-acting neighbors got to work building a pedestrian footbridge. Hilary Canty of the Orcas Island Community Foundation did some quick organizing and volunteers at Island Rides began shuttling people to work and the store as road crews started rebuilding on the double.

Community gatherings are what make living on Orcas Island uniquely wonder-filled. Top left: Beloved and prolific dance instructor Tiffany Loney taught Eirann Cohen and Tika Thorson how to stilt-walk when they were young troupe performers, and they're still doing it as adults in the Annual Summer Solstice Parade in Eastsound, one of our biggest festivities. Another is Island Hardware's Annual Anniversary Sale Day Celebration, complete with a barbecue for all attendees, live music by local musicians, tape-measuring and nail-hammering competitions, and cement stepping-stone decorating, above. It's been a tradition for more than half a century.

Locals remember Jami Ann Sanders' maple bacon donuts at the Village Green Farmers' Market years ago. Lisa Bronn prepares apples for cider pressing and other festivities at Mimi Anderson and Steve Diepenbrock's annual fall gathering at Morning Star Farm in 2013. School groups often sell tempting goodies outside Island Market where shoppers give generously to their causes. Thanksgiving feels extra special at the Odd Fellows Hall, left, an annual tradition in which locals pack the place to share in a gigantic potluck. The Orcas Island Rowing Team hosts the Annual Polar Bear Plunge, right, at Cascade Lake on New Year's Day.

Note to Fellow Islanders

How difficult it is to show only a tiny percentage of our island's people in a book with limited space. And to write a mere caption about each one! If only this could be a thousand pages. You are all important. You all contribute to the heart of this island. You do intriguing things with your lives, create amazing art, hone amazing talents, and fill important needs. It is ever-inspiring to observe and converse with each and every one of you in daily life. Know that you *all* belong in here.

Note to Readers Elsewhere

If you've never been here, what you see in these pages is but a tiny representation of the phenomenal uniquenesses, gatherings, and celebrations we are all accustomed to experiencing. If you find yourself smitten with this life, please set your intentions to graciously respect the island's slow pace and slow growth. This book is not meant to attract an audience, but to document our eccentric rural life as we know and love it.

Final Note to Everyone

I encourage you to do the things you've always wanted to do, wherever you are. The niche for this book has existed ever since we first came here as tourists in 2005, when I wished I had a book about Orcas Island to take home and one to send to my mom. I toyed with the idea of making one since we moved here in 2012, and set it aside each year for various reasons—some of which were very real time constraints due to homeschooling through the years, and others were imagined obstacles. Time went on, our kids went to school, and one day in late summer of 2021, a friend challenged me to let go of the imagined obstacles I was still hanging onto. I did. I dove into the making of this book and found that none of those assumed obstacles materialized. There were times when certain doors closed, but each time better ones opened in their place. Wherever you are—a quiet rural town or a big, bustling city—revisit the dreams you've set aside. Are the obstacles in your way real or imagined? If the latter, I encourage you to let go of them and see what happens when you live out what you feel pulled to do. The world needs your gifts, and will enjoy the fruits of your specific talents and passions. Orcas Island and its people have taught me that.

May the elements you resonate with in this book inspire you to live life to the fullest in your community, connecting with your passions, your neighbors, and the beauty that is around you every day.

So Sincerely, *Edee Kulper*

Ashley Berger basks in the serenity of her dreamy surroundings. Following page: One of the many paintings done by students on Salmonberry School's fence.

Thank you

Mom and Dad, for loving me so well and encouraging me to live out my dreams. I won the lottery with you two.

Evan and Levi, for a magical motherhood that I wouldn't trade for the world. May you live out your dreams too.

Kayleigh Jankowski, for being on this book journey with me every step of the way. You have worked exceedingly professionally, and your skill has made this experience one of pure joy for me. Thank you for your commitment to excellence, more than I can ever say. You are a phenom.

Donna Lane, for giving me peace of mind that was unparalleled. The thought of error was one of my biggest fears in imagining making this book. Thank you for your keen eye, your ever-prompt responses, and your lovely communication. I'm so glad I found you.

Molly Johnson, for keeping me connected with "saying it how Edee would say it." You provided many essential constructive criticisms to ponder and evaluate, and that's what makes a better author. Thank you immensely for not holding back, my friend.

Michael Royse, for your kind legal counsel. It's ever so comforting to have expert advice when doing a project that shows the lives of hundreds of people.

Michelle Gregg, for telling me you'd read every word I wrote if I started the blog that preceded this book. That was a pivotal moment in Sequel; as you were speaking, there was a sweater looking at me that said, "I Can and I Will." Timely words are powerful.

Liz Stangle, for the three words you said when I was waffling over writing this: "Perfection is stagnation." That was what I needed to hear to get going and not let the desire for excellence actually stifle me from putting one foot in front of the other.

Orcas Island Library and librarians, for providing me with a lovely home away from home. As Enzo's was my husband's version of *Cheers*, the library is mine.

Orcas Islanders, for your authentic individuality and caring community. I love being a fly on the wall, documenting who you are and how well you love.

Love one another.
JOHN 13:34

Love never fails.
1 CORINTHIANS 13:8

And for the physically, emotionally, and politically difficult times . . .

When a man's ways are pleasing to the Lord, he makes even his enemies live at peace with him.
PROVERBS 16:7

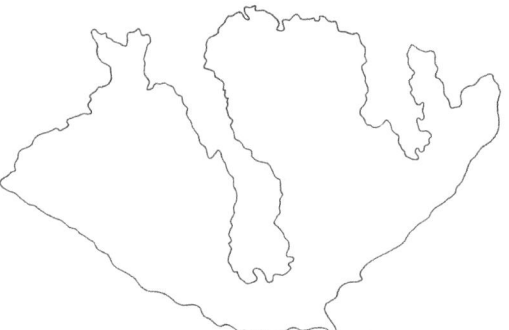